Copyright © 2023 by Thomas Crawford

All rights reserved. No part of this book may be reproduced in any form or by any electronic or mechanical means, including information storage and retrieval systems, without permission in writing from the publisher, except by reviewers, who may quote brief passages in a review.

This publication contains the opinions and ideas of its author. It is intended to provide helpful and informative material on the subjects addressed in the publication. The author and publisher specifically disclaim all responsibility for any liability, loss or risk, personal or otherwise, which is incurred as a consequence, directly or indirectly, of the use and application of any of the contents of this book.

WORKBOOK PRESS LLC
187 E Warm Springs Rd
Suite B285 Las Vegas NV 89119 USA

Website: https://workbookpress.com/
Hotline: 1-888-818-4856
Email: admin@workbookpress.com

Ordering Information:
Quantity sales. Special discounts are available on quantity purchases by corporations, associations, and others.

For details, contact the publisher at the address above.

ISBN-13:   978-1-952754-28-9 (Paperback Version)
              978-1-952754-29-6 (Digital Version)

REV. DATE: 03/18/2024

An artist's study of

MASTER SELF-PORTRAITS

THOMAS CRAWFORD

For our grandchildren, Mahlon, Carlo, Elodie and Wescott

Love,

Crawdad

INTRODUCTION

This little book is the result of an attempt by a painter to study master artists by copying their self-portraits. Painting the portraits and producing the book was enjoyable and, I believe, illuminating. I would recommend the exercise to other painters, particularly young artists, as a way to learn about the great artists, their styles and techniques of painting, and of their works more generally. The exercise may be humbling and of value in revealing differences between any superficial likeness of the copy and the depth and skill of the original.

The three greatest painters, in my opinion, Giotto, Leonardo da Vinci and Michelangelo, did not (so far as we know) paint self-portraits. Leonardo made a well-known and well-preserved pen and ink drawing and Michelangelo painted his visage in the distorted features of St. Bartholomew the Martyr, flayed alive and carrying his own skin, in the Sistine Chapel Last Judgment. Caravaggio, a masterful artist with a reputation for violence, painted his face on the severed head of Goliath in what is surely the most grotesque self-portrait. Rembrandt painted more than seventy self-portraits, Frida Kahlo more than fifty. Durer, perhaps the greatest of all self-portraitists, painted several and did a magnificent silver-point drawing of himself at age thirteen.

Just as self-portraiture is arguably the most subjective of all art forms, so is the viewing of self- portraits and the attraction to particular works highly subjective. My own favorites, Masaccio, Titian, Mantegna, Tiepolo, Matisse and Beckmann, probably reflect my personal preferences for their works. I would like to see and to copy self-portraits of Piero della Francesca and Signorelli, if any exist. And, if I pursue this pleasurable exercise further, I would like to track down and copy other favorites, Fra Angelico, Vermeer, Otto Dix and Edward Hopper.

May young artists who encounter this book be inspired to copy the masters for the sheer pleasure and edification it would likely bring them.

–Thomas Crawford

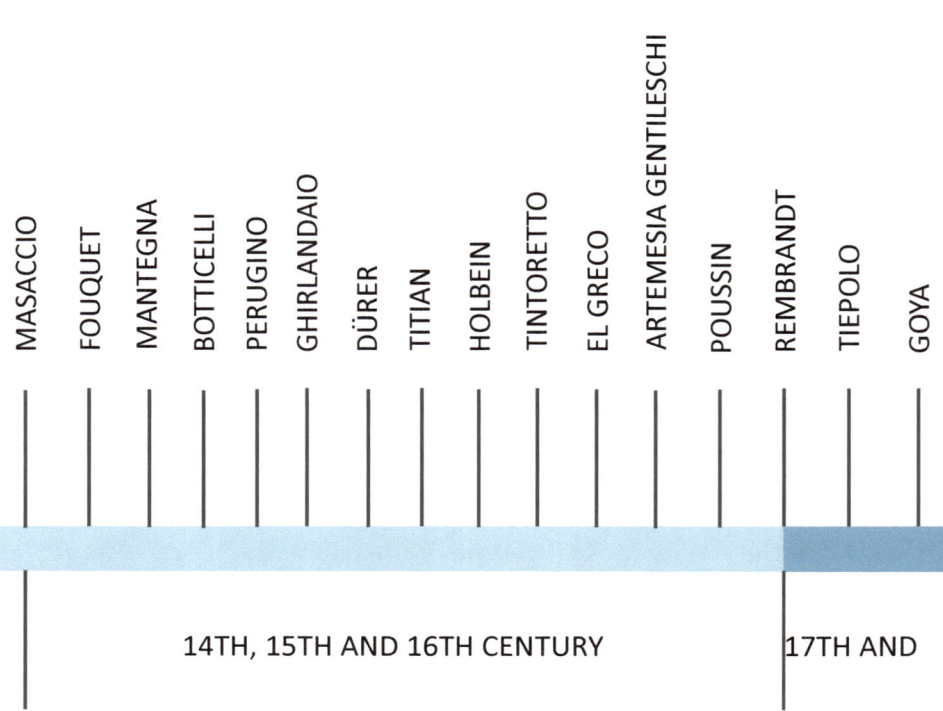

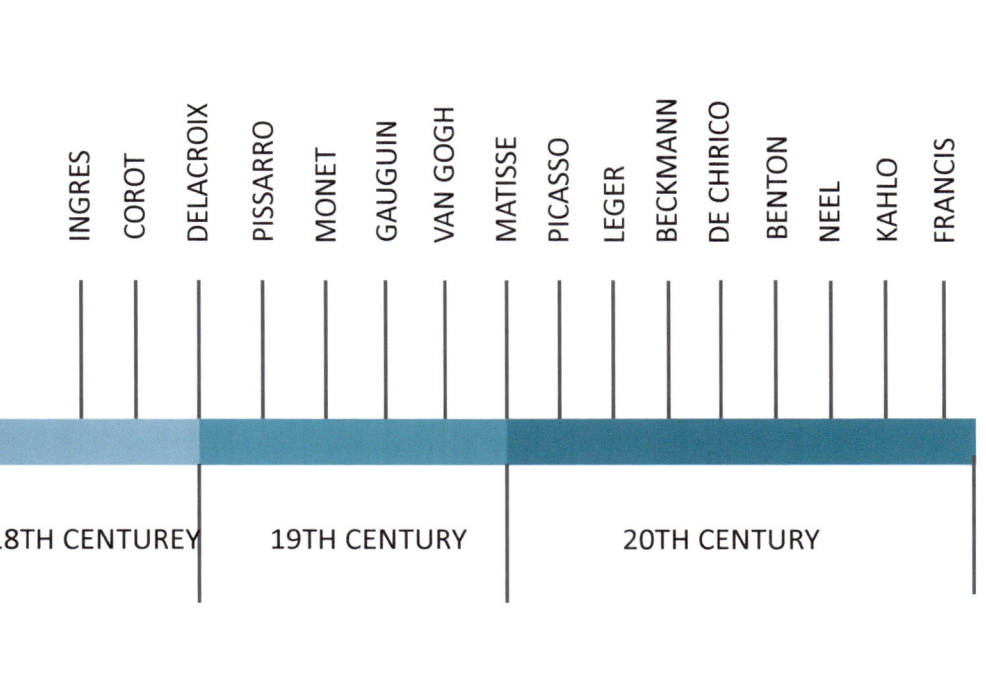

TOMMASO DI GIOVANNI GUIDI,
called **MASACCIO**

B 1401, Italy
d. 1428, Rome
portrait from *The Tribute Money*,
1425-28 (age: 24-26)
Brancacci Chapel, Santa Maria del Carmine, Florence

After Giotto and Fra Angelico, Masaccio is generally considered to be the greatest painter of the early Italian Renaissance. His figures have a heroic quality and dignity that is particularly obvious in his best-known works, *Adam and Eve Cast out of the Paradise* and *The Tribute Money*, two panels in the Brancacci Chapel, Florence.

Other notable masterpieces are *St. Peter and St. john Distributing Alms* (Brancacci Chapel); Crucifixion, (Pinacoteca, Naples) and *The Most Holy Trinity* (Basilica Santa Maria Novella, Florence).

JEAN FOUQUET

b. about 1420, Tours, France
d. 1481, Tours
self-portrait, enamel painting,
about 1450 (gae, 30)
Louvre, Paris

The greatest of the early French masters, Jean Fouquet is believed to have studied and been influenced by Fra Angelico. His best paitings are probably a miniature, *David given Tidings of the Death of Saul,* (Bibliotheque Nationale, Paris) *Pieta* (Parish Church, Nouans, Indre-et-Loire); and *Virgin and Child* (Melun Diptych, Musee Royal des Beaux-Arts, Antwerp).

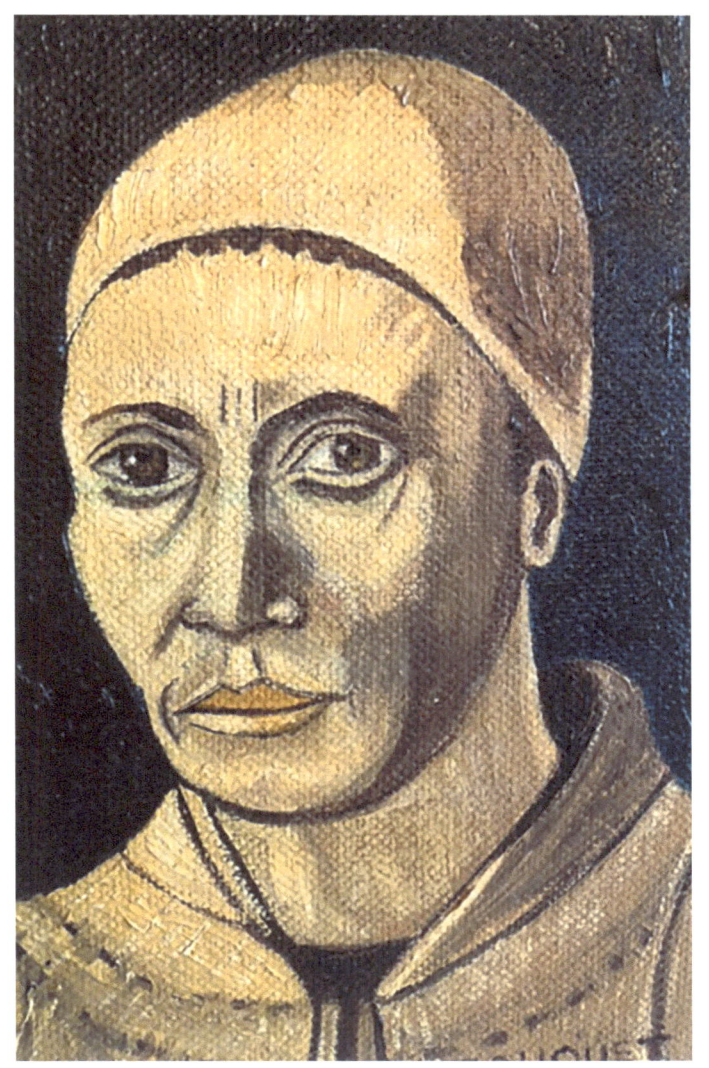

ANDREA MANTEGNA

born 1431, Isola di Carturo, Italy
died 1506, Mantua, Italy
self-portrait from fresco of St. James before Herod Agrippa, 1457 (age, 26)
Overtari Chapel, Erimitani Church, Padua

Mantegna is justly famed for the combination of expressive power and accomplished craftmanship in his paintings. He married the daughter of Jacopo Bellini and thus became the brother-in-law of Giovanni Bellini, whose paintings are among the most powerful of the Italian Renaissance: *Dead Christ* (Brera Museum, Milan); *The Crucifixion* (Louvre, Paris); and *St. Sebastian* (Louvre). Also notable is *Madonna of the Victory* (Louvre).

SANDRO DI FILIPEPI,
called **BOTTICELLI**

born 1445, Florence, Italy
died 1510, Florence, Italy
self-portrair from Adopation of
the Magi, 1476 (age, 31)
Uffizi, Florence

When still a boy, Botticelli entered the workshop of Filippo Lippi and later when he established his own workshop he employed his former teacher's son, Filippino Lippi, as an assistant. Among Botticelli's best known and admired works are *Primavera* (Uffizi, Florence): *Birth of Venus* (Uffizi); *St. Augustine* (Ognissanti, Florence); and *Miracles of St. Zenobias* (National Gallery, London).

PIETRO VANUCCI,
called **PERUGINO**

born,1445, Citta Della Pieve, Umbria, Italy
self-portrait, date of painting unknown
Colefgio del Cambrio, Perugia

Perugino apprenticed in Verrocchio's workshop alongside
Leonardo, Ghirlandaio, Lorenzo di Credi and Filippino Lippi. He is said to be one of the earliest Italian oil painters. However, his most famous work is a fresco in the Sistine Chapel, *The Handing of the Keys to St. Peter*. Other major paintings are *Pieta* (Uffizi); *Crucifixion* (Santa Maria Maddalena dei Pazzi, Florence) and *Madonna and Saints* (Louvre).

DOMENICO GHIRLANDAIO

born 1449, Florence, Italy.
died 1494, Florence.
Portrait from The Adoration of the Shepherds, 1485-86,(age, 36-37)
Sassetti Chapel,
Santa Trinita, Florence.

Ghirlandaio ran the leading painting studio in Florence in the late 15th century and among his many students was Michaelangelo. He excelled in the painting of murals and had a particular talent for depicting contemporary life and portraits of contemporary people within the context of religious narratives. Among his notable works are *The Adoration of the Shepherds, The Last Supper* (Ognissanti, Florence) and two magnificent portraits, *Giovanna Tornabuoni* (Museo Thyssen-Bornemisza, Madrid) and *Portrait of an Old Man with his Grandson* (Louvre Museum, Paris).

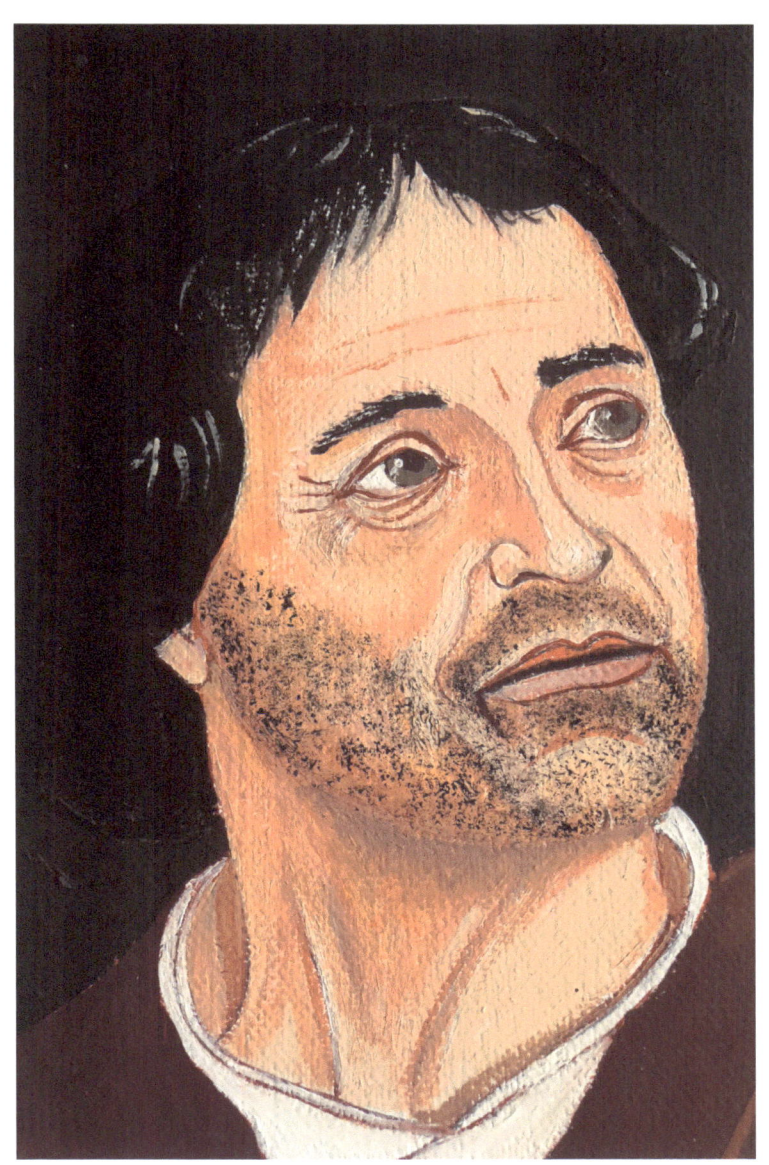

ALBRECHT DÜRER

born 1471, Nuremberg, Germany.
died 1528, Nuremberg
self-portrait, 1498 (age, 27)
Prado, Madrid

Dürer has been called the father of the self-portrait, an appropriate appellation when one considers the masterful
silverpoint drawing he did at age 13 (on public view at Graphische Sammlung Albertina, Vienna) and the three self-portraits in oil that he completed before he was 30, housed in the Louvre, Prado, and Alte Pinakothek, Munich. Other reknowned works are *The Four Apostles* (Alte Pinakothek,), *The Adoration of the Magi*, (Uffizi), *Young Venetian Woman* (Kunsthistorisches Museum, Vienna); a watercolor and gouache, *Hare* (Graphische Sammlung Albertina); and a copperplate engraving, *Knight, Death and the Devil* (Staatliche Museen zu Berlin).

TIZIANO VECELLIO, called **TITIAN**

born 1485-88, Pieve di Cadore,
died 1576, Venice
self-portrait, about 1565 (age 80)
Museo del Prado, Madrid

Titian was such a versatile master of portraits, landscapes and mythological and religious subjects that his contemporaries recognized him, it is said, as "the sun amidst small stars." His portraits of *Pietro Aretino* (Frick Collection, New York) and *Portrait of Riminaldi* (Pitti Gallery, Florence) are among the first group of greatest portraits. In *The Assumption of the Virgin* (Santa Maria dei Frari, Venice) Titian treats this subject with unequalled splendor and majesty, just as he does *The Entombment* (Louvre). His celebrated nudes include *Danae* (Prado) and *Sacred and Profane Love* (Borghese Gallery, Rome).

HANS HOLBEIN

born 1497, Augsburg, Holy Roman Empire
died 1543, London
self-portrait, colored chalk-drawing, date unknown
Uffizi, Florence

Holbein is recognized as one of the premier portraitists of his or any time, not only because of his courtly subjects but because of the careful and precise execution of his art. Among his best portraits are those of *Henry VIII* (one at Thyssen-Bornemisza Museum, Madrid, and the other at
Whitehall, England), *Sir Thomas More* (Frick Collection, New York), double portrait of Jean de Dinteville and Georges de Selve called *The Ambassadors* (National Gallery, London) and *Erasmus of Rotterdam* (Longfond Castle, England).

JACOPO ROBUSTI,
called **TINTORETTO**

born 1518, Venice, Italy.
died 1594, Venice
self-portrait, around 1588 (age, 70).
Louvre, Paris

Tintoretto, a student of Titian's for only a brief period, was nonetheless influenced by his teacher and was said to have nailed a sign to his workshop door reading, "Michelangelo's drawing, Titian's color." He succeeded in part by the precise rendering of bodies in movement that he so consistently achieved. Titian's influence is apparent in his splendid Susanna and the Elders (Gemaldegalerie, Vienna). Tintoretto's fame justly rests on the cycle of pictures he painted for more than 20 years in the Scuola di San Rocco, Venice. Three particular masterpieces in that vast body of work are The Crucifixion, Christ before Pilate, and The Way to Golgotha.

ARTEMISIA GENTILESCHI

born July 8, 1593, Rome, Italy
died 1653, Naples, Italy

Artemisia Gentileschi is the most celebrated female painter of the 17th century. Her highly successful international career featured commissions in Rome, Florence, Venice, Naples and London. An admirer of the work of Caravaggio and her father, Orazio, her paintings were among the most dramatic and dynamic of the Baroque period. Among her greatest paintings are *Judith Slaying Holofernes* (1620); *Lucretia* (1623-25) and *Cleopatra* (1633-35). *The Duomo of Pozzuoli* (Naples) contains early paintings by her.

DOMINICOS THEOTOCOPULI, called **EL GRECO**

born 1541, Fodele, Crete. died 1614, Toledo, Spain self-portrait, 1610 (age, 69) Metropolitan Museum, New York

El Greco was born and spent his youth in Crete before migrating to Venice, spending some time in Rome, then living the last 37 years of his life in Toledo. Among his masterpieces are *St. Jerome* (Frick Collection, New York); *Portrait of Covarrubias* (Louvre, Paris); and *Toledo in a Storm* (Metropolitan Museum, New York).

NICOLAS POUSSIN

born 1594, Villers, France died 1665, Rome, Italy
self-portrait, 1650 (age, 56)
Louvre, Paris

Poussin, a cultured man drawn to classical studies, painted in what could be considered a neo-classical style. He took up painting relatively late and, unusual for a Frenchman, he went to Rome to study and spent most of his active life there. Among his most notable works are *The Massacre of the Innocents* (Musee Conde, Chantilly); *The Martyrdom of St. Erasmus* (Pinacoteca Vaticana, Vatican City); and *Apollo and Daphne* (Louvre, Paris).

REMBRANDT HARMENSZ VAN RIJN

born 1606, Leyden, Holland
died 1669 Amsterdam
self-portrait, 1657 (age, 60)
Kunsthistorisches Museum,
Cologne, Germany.

Rembrandt was the most prolific self-portraitist of all; about 70 paintings and 30 etchings survive. But, he was not the greatest, considering the magnificent four self-portraits of Dürer. Among his masterpieces in other genre are *The Night Watch* (Rijksmuseum, Amsterdam); *The Polish Rider* (Frick Collection, New York); *The Supper at Emmaus* (Louvre); *Danae* (Hermitage, Leningrad); and *Bathsheba* (Louvre).

GIAMBATTISTA TIEPOLO

born 1696, Venice, Italy
died 1770, Madrid, Spain
self-portrait in ceiling fresco,
1753 (age, 57)
Prince-Archbishops Palace,
Wurzburg

Tiepolo, one of the greatest decorative artists ever, was the premier ceiling painter of the 18th century. His son, Domenico, studied and worked with his father and maintained the family's pre-eminence in decorative painting. Among Giambattista Tiepolo's masterpieces are the canvases *Scourge of the Serpents* (Gallerie dell' Academia, Venice) and *Neptune Offering to Venice the Riches of the Sea* (Palazzo Ducale, Venice); and frescoes *Sara and the Angel* (Archbishop's Palace, Udine) and *The Carrying of the Holy House from Nazareth to Loretto* (Gallerie dell'Academia), and scenes of America and Africa from the fresco on the ceiling of the staircase (Wurzburg, Residenz, Germany).

FRANCISCO JOSE DE GOYA Y LUCIENTES

born 1746, Fuentetodos, Spain
died 1828, Bordeaux, France
self-portrait, 1815 (age, 69)
Prado, Madrid

Goya was as good a portraitist as he was a fierce realist, whether depicting royalty, the common man or the brutality of war. *The Nude Maja*, a painting of the Duchess of Alba, is one of the most celebrated of all nudes (Prado, Madrid); *The Execution - May 3, 1808* (Prado) indicts that and all similar militaristic evils; *The Forge* is a tribute to the
working man (Frick Collection, New York).

JEAN-AUGUSTE-DOMINGUE INGRES

born 1780, Montauban, France
died 1867, Paris
self-portrait, 1804 (age, 24)
Musee Conde, Chantilly

Ingres, David's greatest pupil, is revered for his meticulous draftsmanship and refined but unsentimental portraiture. Examples of his best work can be seen at the Louvre, *Odalisque and Mme Riviere*; at Hermitage, Leningrad, *Portrait of Count Guryev*; and in the Frick Collection, New York, *Comtesse d'Haussonville.*

JEAN-BAPTIST-CAMILLE COROT

born 1796, Paris, France
died 1875, Paris
self-portrait, about 1835 (age, 39)
Uffizi, Florence

As an art student in Rome, Corot studied nature and light effects rather than copying classical works. His landscapes and seascapes reflect this lyrical approach and can be viewed as precursors of Impressionism. Notable works include *Belfry of Douai, The Bridge at Narni*, and *Venise, La Piazetta,* all at the Louvre, and *La Rochelle* (Collection of Stephen C. Clark, New York).

EUGENE DELACROIX

born 1798, Ile-de-France, France
died 1863, Paris
self-portrait, 1860 (age, 62)
Uffizi, Florence

Delacroix, leader of the French Romantic school, was inspired by Rubens and painters of the Venetian Renaissance and influenced by his friend and contemporary, Theodore Gericault. His most notable works include *Liberty Leading the People, The Barque of Dante, Massacre at Chios, and Death of Sardanapalus* (all at the Louvre).

CAMILLE PISSARRO

born 1830, St. Thomas, Virgin Islands
died 1903, Paris
self-portrait, 1873 (age, 43)
Musee d'Orsay, Paris

Pissarro, born in the Virgin Islands, left home for Paris after
25 years and never returned. Yearning for a simpler life, he left Paris for rural areas, first Pontoise and then Louveciennes but maintained his ties to the Parisian cultural elite. He and Monet prepared what was to become the first Impressionist exhibition in 1874 and continued the practice with other early Impressionists, Renoir and Sisley. Known as an encouraging mentor of young artists he invited Gauguin, Signac and Seurat to participate in later exhibitions. Celebrated for his landscapes and rustic scenes, among his best works are *The Lock on the Seine at Bougival* (Marion & Henry Block Collection); *The Wash House, Bougival* (Musee d'Orsay, Paris); *The Seine at Port-Marley* (Staatsgalerie, Stuttgart).

CLAUDE MONET

born 1840, Le Havre, France
died 1926, Giverny, France
self-portrait, 1886 (age, 46)
Rijksmuseum, Amsterdam

Monet credits Eugene Boudin and the Dutch painter Johan Jongkind as his most important teachers. One of his paintings shown at the first Impressionist exhibition, *Impression, Sunrise*, led critics to coin the term "Impressionist" to describe the group's collective style. Monet was brilliantly productive at the sites of three homes, in a town on the Seine, Argenteuil, in the village of Vetheuil, and in his Normandy property, Giverny. Among his masterpieces are *Fishermen on the Seine at Poissy* (Osterreichische Galerie, Vienna); *Autumn on the Seine, Argenteuil* (Mrs. John Hay Whitney Collection); *The Basin at Argenteuil* (Museum of Art, Rhode Island School of Design) Providence, Rhode Island; *Impression Sunrise* (Musee Marmottan, Paris) and *Water Lillies* (Pinakotek, Munich).

PAUL GAUGUIN

born 1848, Paris, France
died 1903, Atuona, Marquesas Islands, French Polynesia
self-portrait, 1890 (age, 51)
Musee d'Orsay, Paris

Gauguin was 18 months old when his family left Paris for Peru. His father died on the voyage leaving his young family to fend for themselves in Lima for four years before returning to France. Gauguin's childhood encounters with Pre-Columbian pottery was said to have influenced his mature art. He became a stockbroker at age 23 and worked as a successful Parisian businessman for eleven years. During that time he began to paint, made friends with Pissarro, who mentored him and introduced him to other artists, including Cezanne. In 1887 he painted in Martinique; in 1888 he spent nine weeks in Arles painting with Van Gogh; in 1891 he went to Tahiti for the first time; then after a stay in Paris, in 1895 he traveled again to Tahiti, never to return to Europe. Among his most important works are *Where Do We Come From? What are we? Where Are We Going?* (1897, Museum of Fine Arts, Boston); The Yellow Christ (1889) Albright-Knox Art Gallery, Buffalo, NY); The Seed of the Areoi (1892, The Museum of Modern Art, New York); and Spirit of the Dead Watching (1892, Albright-Knox Art Gallery).

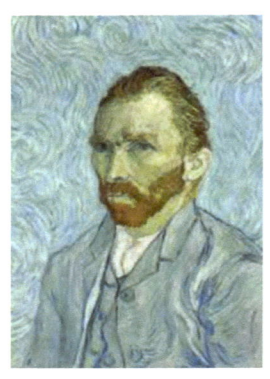

VINCENT VAN GOGH

born 1853, Groot Zundert, Holland
died 1890, Auvers-sur-Oise, France
self-portrait, 1889 (age, 36)
Musee d'Orsay

Van Gogh was 27 when he decided to be a painter. He took his own life 10 years later. During that brief period he developed from a draftsman of grim scenes of the poor and oppressed to become the father of modern Expressionism and a painter of extreme originality whose distinctive brush strokes and vibrant palette seemed to be influenced by no one or nothing but Van Gogh himself. Among his masterpieces are Pere Tanguy (Collection Stavros Niarchos, Athens); *L'Arlesienne* (Metropolitan Museum of Art, New York); *The Starry Night* (Museum of Modern Art, New York); *The Road Menders* (Cleveland Museum of Art).

HENRI MATISSE

born 1869, Cateau, France
died 1954, Nice, France
self-portrait, 1906 (age, 37)
Statens Museum for Kunst,
Copenhagen

Few would disagree that Matisse, along with Picasso, is the most important and influential artist of the twentieth century. He is known everywhere and millions of reproductions of his works decorate homes, offices and hotels. Considered the father of "fauvism," a style of painting using broad, strong areas of pure color, Matisse has influenced Expressionism and Cubism and other succeeding styles. Notable works include *Madame Matisse* (The Hermitage, St. Petersburg) *The Green Line* (Statens Museum for Kunst, Copenhagen); *Black and Gold Nude* (Hermitage Museum, St. Petersburg); *The Window* (Detroit Institute of Arts, Detroit); and *Still Life of Oranges* (Musee Picasso, Paris).

PABLO PICASSO

born 1881, Malaga, Spain
died 1973, Mougins, France
self-portrait, 1906 (age, 25)
Philadelphia Museum of Art

In terms of sheer quantity, Picasso may be the most productive painter ever, and the variety of styles in that vast production is equally awe-inspiring. His Cubist works (a style developed by Picasso and Braque) are but one class along with his "classical" and "blue period" works. The variety of his genius can be seen in these paintings: *Portrait of Pedro Manach* (National Gallery of Art, Washington, D.C.); *Poor People at the Beach* (National Gallery of Art. Washington, D.C.); *Woman in White* (Metropolitan Museum of Art, New York); *Les Demoiselles d'Avignon* (Metropolitan Museum of Art, New York); *Deux Femmes Courant sur la Plage and Portrait of Dora Maar* (both at Musee Picasso, Paris); and *Guernica* (Museo Nacional Centro de Arte Reina Sofia, Madrid).

FERNAND LEGER

born 1881, Orne, France,
died 1955, Gif-sur-Yvette, France
self-portrait, 1953 (age, 72)
Collection Raimondo Rezzonico,
Locarno, Switzerland

Leger lived on his father's cattle farm in lower Normandy until he was 18, when he began training as an architect. He moved to Paris and supported himself as an architectural draftsman before doing his military service, then attended Beaux-Arts as a non-enrolled student. He did not work seriously as a painter until age 25. Within four years he exhibited his work with other young artists recognized as "Cubists." His career was interrupted by four years of service with the French Army during World War I, an experience that resulted in work in which figures and objects were rendered in machinelike forms. His style took on traits of Le Corbusier's Purism, which utilized structured, mechanical matrices upon which figures and objects were placed. Later, organic and irregular forms assumed greater importance. Throughout his career he depicted the common man and his world in bold contours. Among his most notable masterpieces are *Acrobats and Musicians* (Galerie Aime Maeght, Paris), *Three Musicians* (Museum of Modern Art, New York), *Man with a Blue Hat* (Musee National Fernand Leger, Biot, France), *Two Sisters* (Staaliche Museen Preussischer Kulturbesitz, Nationalgalerie, Berlin) and *Nude on a Red Background* (Hirshorn Museum, Smithsonian, Washington, D.C.).

MAX BECKMANN

born 1884, Leipzig, Germany
died 1950, New York
self-portrait, 1944 (age, 60)
Neue Staatsgalerie, Munich

Beckmann is celebrated for his self-portraits painted throughout his life. He had great success and official honors during the Weimar Republic teaching in Frankfurt. However, the Nazi government labeled him "a cultural Bolshevik" and in 1933 dismissed him from his teaching position. In 1937 the government confiscated more than 500 of his works. He left Germany and began a self-imposed exile in Amsterdam, where he lived in poverty for 10 years before immigrating to America. His works include *The Bark* (National Gallery, Berlin); *Self-portrait with a Horn* (Collection Ronald Lauder); *The Night* (Kunstsammlung Nordrheim-Westfalen, Dusseldorf).

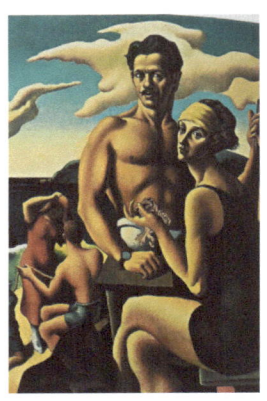

THOMAS HART BENTON

born April 15,1889, Neosho, Missouri
died January 19, 1975, Kansas City, Missouri

Thomas Hart Benton, American painter, muralist and print maker, was the leader of the regionalist art movement that included Grant Wood and John Steurart Curry. He mentored the renowned abstract painter, Jackson Pollack. Benton illustrated several of America's most enduring books including Mark Twain's Huckleberry Finn, Tom Sawyer, Life on the Mississippi, and John Steinbeck's The Grapes of Wrath.

GIORGIO DE CHIRICO

born 1888, Volos, Greece died 1978, Rome, Italy
self-portrait, 1939 (age, 51)
Collection Raimondo Rezzonico, Lucerne, Switzerland

Born in Greece of Italian parents, De Chirico studied art in Athens and Florence before moving to Germany and entering the Academy of Fine Arts in Munich. He read and was impressed by the writings of German philosophers Nietzche and Schopenhauer. After moving back to Italy he painted the first of his "Metaphysical Town Square" series. When he visited Turin on his way to Paris, he was deeply moved by what he called the "metaphysical aspect" of Turin, the architecture of its archways and piazzas. Not surprisingly, De Chirico is best known for the haunted, brooding moods evoked by images of his "metaphysical" canvases. Among his major works are *The Red Tower* (Peggy Guggenheim Collection, Venice), *Love Song* (Museum of Modern Art, New York), *The Philosopher* (Philadelphia Museum of Art), and *The Disquieting Muses* (University of Iowa Museum of Art).

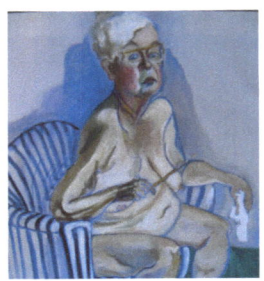

ALICE NEEL

born 1900 Merion Square, Pennsylvania
died 1984, New York, NY
self-potrait, 1980 (age 80)
National Portrait Gallery,
Smithsonian Institution,
Washington, D.C.

Neel was raised in a strict middle-class family which she helped support with clerical work before she enrolled in the Philadelphia School of Design for Women. One year before graduating she married a Cuban graduate art student then moved to Havana to live with her husband's family. She was embraced by the Cuban avant-garde art community and developed her painting. The trauma caused by the death her first child at age one deeply affected Neel, whose work, thereafter, was infused with themes of loss, motherhood and anxiety. Her second child was born within year and taken away by her father to Cuba. Neel mourned the loss of her husband and daughter and suffered a massive nervous breakdown. She was placed in the suicide ward of a Philadelphia hospital where she continued to paint and eventually recovered.

During the Depression, Neel was one of the first artists to work for the Works Progress Administration. After the war her works gained critical recognition. Two notable wor *Kitty Pearson* and *Dominican Boys on 108th Street*, are both in the Tate Collection London. Her paintings are in major museum collections, including the Fine Arts Museums of San Francisco, Boston and Houston, National Gallery of Art, Washington D.C., Art Institute of Chicago, Metropolitan Museum of Art, New York, and Modern Museet, Stockholm.

FRIDA KAHLO

born 1907 Coyocan, Mexico
died 1954, Coyocan
Self-Portrait with Thorn Necklace and Hummingbird, 1940 (age, 33)
Harry Hanson Center, UT, Austin, Texas

Kahlo contracted polio as a child and suffered serious injuries in her teens as a result of a traffic accident. Of at least 140 paintings she created 55 are self-portraits. She is reported to have said, "I paint myself because I am so often alone and because I am the subject I know best." Suggestions of pain are present in many of her works owing to her illnesses, injuries, several miscarriages and a very troubled marriage to her mentor, painter Diego Rivera. Among her most notable paintings are: *The Frame* (Louvre, Paris); *Self-portrait with Cropped Hair* (Museum of Modern Art, New York); *Diego on My Mind* (Collection Jacques and Natasha Gelman); *The Fruits of the Earth* (Collection Banco Nacional de Mexico, Mexico City).

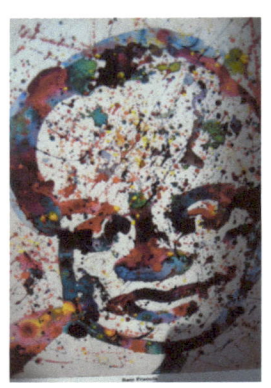

SAM FRANCIS

born 1923, San Mateo, California
died 1994, Santa Monica, California
self-portrait, 1976 (age, 53)
Collection, E.W.K., Berne, Switzerland

Francis served in the U.S. Air Force during World War II before being injured in test flight maneuvers. He was hospitalized for several years and during that time began to paint. After recovering he attended the University of California, Berkeley where he received both a BA and MA degree. He was influenced by abstract expressionists Rothko, Gorky and Still. In the 1950s he lived and worked in Paris and from there traveled to Tokyo, Mexico City, Bern and New York, where he established studios. In the 1960s and until his death he painted mostly in Los Angeles and Tokyo. Among his notable works are *Black and Red* (Contemporary Museum, Honolulu), *Blue* (The Phillips Collection, Washington, D.C.), *Big Red, Towards Disappearance II*, and *Moby Dick* (all at the Museum of Modern Art, New York).

www.ingramcontent.com/pod-product-compliance
Lightning Source LLC
Chambersburg PA
CBHW042039050526
44107CB00107B/1037